Sun in the golden Chariot('Hiranyaena Sabita Rathena) by Praharaj, is a priceless treasure in our literature.
- **Justice Harihar Mohapatra**

Praharaj holds a lofty position amongst leading contemporary odia poets.
- **Sachi Routray**

-The Bhavan's Journal:
Nanda's inspiration is vedic Upanishadic. But he is very much contemporaneous and speaks out unhesitatingly against man-made violence.
- Dr Prem Nandakumar

-The Skylark India:
Every poem is seasoned with mystical flavour which demands the deep insight and certain fund of spiritual knowledge of the readers in advance for the very ecstasy of intellectual interpretation.
- **Nar Deo Sharma**

The Mahanadi Review:
Each poem not withstanding the nature of its etheme is an extremely neat composition.
- **Bibhu Padhi**

Triveni:
Unfailingly conveys the lilt and music of the original.
- V K Tonpo

The Indian Pen:
No poem is more than ten lines long and presumes to deal with ultimates, such as birth, death and destruction, the quality of Truth, childhood etc.
- Havovi Anklesaria

The Prativa India:
The voice is one of a sensitive tortured soul.
- Prof Ranga Kapoor

The Poetry:
Every poem is a metaphoric journey into the all pervasive Atman. The poems wear imagistic texture.
- B C Mohanty

Sun in the Golden Chariot

Sun in the Golden Chariot
'Hiranyayena Sabita Rathena'

Praharaj Satyanarayan Nanda

(Translated By The Poet)

BLACK EAGLE BOOKS
Dublin, USA | Bhubaneswar, India

Black Eagle Books
USA address:
7464 Wisdom Lane
Dublin, OH 43016

India address:
E/312, Trident Galaxy, Kalinga Nagar,
Bhubaneswar-751003, Odisha, India

E-mail: info@blackeaglebooks.org
Website: www.blackeaglebooks.org

First International Edition Published by
Black Eagle Books, 2023

SUN IN THE GOLDEN CHARIOT
by **Praharaj Satyanarayan Nanda**
(Translated By The Poet)

Copyright © Praharaj Satyanarayan Nanda

All rights reserved. No part of this publication may be reproduced, stored in a retrieval system, or transmitted, in any form or by any means, electronic, mechanical, photocopying, recording or otherwise without the prior permission of the publisher.

Cover & Interior Design: Ezy's Publication

ISBN- 978-1-64560-374-0 (Paperback)

Printed in the United States of America

Dedicated To
Manoj Das
Sri Aurobindo Ashram, Pondicherry

Sri Praharaj Satyanarayan Nanda belongs to a special category in Odia Literature. In all his writings he uses insight to highlight the invisible glow of the outer and mundane world. The logical blending of unconscious and conscious thoughts flourishes in most of his writings. He has made "Many endeavours to explore the meanings from scenes around". This slim volume "HIRANYAYENA SABITA RATHENA" is a new treasure in our literature.

Stoney Road,   **Justice Harihar Mohapatra**
Cuttack-753002
23rd March, 1990

I- THE DOVE ON THE PLAINTAIN LEAF

> The force that through the green fuse,
> drives the flowers,
> Drives my green age,
> That blasts the roots of the trees…..
> Is my destroyer.
>
> -Dylan Thomas

Life emanates from food and from food ensues death.
The offering of rice to *Yagna* flies like a bird,
Moves through the boughs of blue smoke beyond a blue pool
Vibrant desires descend from the wings of clouds
Inscribing the manifesto of action,
Descend the spear-like pourings of water.
And the centre cannot hold instincts of mind;

Earth, covered with green grass, looks blue and glossy
Ah, the glaze of the skin of a child!
And soul, a tossing murky dot, beneath the skull.
A sheaf of November paddy on a *sari* border.
Enwraps your arms.
Ah, you don't enwrap but the sky encompasses you!
Turf, blue and tender, glitters and glows.
The dancing calf clings to its mother with moos,
The dove on a plantain leaf balancing a mouthful of skies,
Lays the legs to ensnare its self in a trap

Why do you come to the veranda, the stairs and the roof tops
You have no axe to grind, no documents in hand.
Why do you loiter keeping off your pair of shoes ?
Will you resort to snags in understanding ?
There is no iron chest, no barn or bamboo- basket
Yet all love weighs heavy on your legs.
You have the tender blue fields, blue reverie,
Have you seen the blue eyes rolling on *Tamala* leaves,

The sketch of a blue hill on broken walls dominating the skyline?
How I sense my physique you don't know
You don't know how wind makes me feel
How the other one experiences its appearance.
The Pull of my body touches the trees and creepers.
You can't fly straight hence you trust in waist
Think of the storm raging in front of you.
Think of the wall resting behind you;
To your left the bough is like a narrow track
Towards the right extend the blue fields
And many a bamboo thicket.
You flow in silence: A strange fall,
Your sighs are spikes of paddy,
Draw sketches here and there
And the wind whirls up the fallen leaves.
Who is your own? the crops, the turfs or the sea of silence?
You yourself link me inside and outside.
The music of sound of life emanates from food:
Waves of sound. Void, a tiny pearl, does not entail anguish on heart.

Golden paddy, basketful and fragrant measured out in units.
The handful of night jasmines.
And the black cowrie eyeballs,
Eyeballs blackened in a conclave basket;
Ah, when do you embody the qualities of a Devi?
Clad in silk you bend your hand head in a little raised altar,
don't coily And hold all assets in your palms.

The sunshine of blue November
And the glance from her rolling eyes
Glitter on blue grooves, gloss of garments.
A physique before the mirror,
The goodness of crops, the stone from Harappa!

You are a monument to eloquence
Ah, an epic half written yet brilliant.

Offering in the plates cocoanut, cakes, delicious sweets
If someone sits in front of you
How can you shirk?
Crops and turfs are like the beauty of body,
What is the force within these,
What's the force?
How food comes to your palms;
How in hunger and thirst and ennui?
Life after life you strive to fill the leather bag,
Butter, cashew and cream jam boost the glaze of skin.

As you pile up crops life emanates
I don't know what craves out eyes, nose, ears
And the quite *Brindavan*.
Although you build the bolts, machine parts
Viewing from outside I discover:
Mother is the primodial father,
The second is food.
Pearl in the conch shell, the yellow in the embryo
Grow up like the delicate form of art day by day.

The blades of grasss, the sesamum and rice
Offered to the *Yagna* return to the earth,
Return the crops;
And to my tongue the tender blue grass,
The lotus stalk to my throat,
The rice juice to the cavity of my heart;
Bone builds the bone stronger,
Flesh sustains the ball of flesh.

The limping king comes to a halt
In hunger, agony or war.

The body with all its bolts and machine parts
A plantain leaf in the wind,
A strange garment flutters;
Kerchief covered round the neck
Clothe hemmed over the feet
Awareness touching the nail-points
And the pores dotted with sweats
Grain that begins to sprout in earth has a sky overhead.

The blue sun of November has lurking mercury dots
Your blue grooves flash in leaves and flowers,
The gloss of ghararas.
Am I the physique or its knowledge or the environs
Eyes fail to measure the rest tenure of longevity,
Neither fat nor flesh, neither skin nor sin.
Ah, what's other than a body!
Greed turns into thirst through the nostrils.

Hooking a long poll I hang in the void
Empty cage has some golden bird within,
My home, my family, my shadow look pretty
My body is not me…. The ephemeral city.

Ah, My Physique!

There lived a lion, a ferocious one,
Named the king *Vasuraka*.
He created havoc in the woods.
All the animals were frightened.
They entreated him together to accept a prey everyday,
Accept like an arranged plate of food.

They requested him not to turn wild in hunger
Not to kill the deer, hares and bears,
"a beast will turn up everyday'
Even before it gets a signal of your zestful swallowing;
Be merciful to all of us;
We, your subjects, intend to live in peace".
The king *Vasuraka* nodded his approval to pacify the beasts.
They chalked out a plan, fixed timing for turning up.
In the morning, a tiny hare trode down the narrow forest lane,
It was shivering in fear,
Covering a little distance it stood near the wall
And looked into water to trace its nice shadow.
While it wasted time in gazing at shadow
The lion turned furious, ran wild,
With furling mane to pounce upon the animal.

At this juncture of time
The hare leaned its cheeks against the palm,

Sought the lion's mercy to save the animals from the wrath of another lion.

Sensing obstruction by the rival
The lion roared and jumped into the well to wage a war.
"Toothless snake, assetless king, powerless elephant are killed.
But the lion living in the fort is all powerful.
He intercepted us on our way emerging into the forest.
O king! The beasts of the jungle seek refuse!"

"If the foe in the fort is ferocious, I am not tactless,
I shall shatter all his pride if you lead me properly"
On the heels of the lion the hare, the wolf, the jackle and the bear moved,
"See the terrible fort and the terrible foe therein".
Said the hare, "O Lord, the wrathful fool lies under the water
Its mare is not raised".
Leaning its neck on the brim of the well the lion roared.
Challenged its opponent and scanned own shadow
Raving deliriously the king, danced and jumped into the well:
"There is no lion in the fort, Oh, I undo my body"

                              -      -   -

For whom the last scene of the tragedy bears fruit?
For whom the beasts danced in zest inveigling against the king
Tumults of a physique ended in infatuation, turned a corpse:
Ah, it floated on the water to woo bees to lunch a fete.
My home, my family and my umbrella are endearing.
I am not the body, a lid of desires.

        * * *

Life emanates from food, the variety of odour;
From the clouds descend the drops,
The bait for an embryo.

Earth is a coiled green snake in sleep,
Ah, you don't know the poet awaits at the entrance

Therefore the sacred urn is filled with his blood
Therefore the little dove dies in its mother's funeral.
Therefore, tying up the calf to the leg of cow
The crafty cowman plays flute from his veranda.
The echoes wander in the grooves.

Bowers hang from the boughs,
The grafts from the branches,
The food you cook abiding the rules
Emits sweetness of honey,
Whats yourself? Food , turf, peace?
You alone can hook up your home and outside.

The blue sun of November has dangling squares in the ear-rings,
And your tiny signature full of fragrance shines on leaves and flowers.

Sighs lovelier than the physique lull you to sleep,
Unaware, you like to walk through many a chamber,
An altar in the kiln, O! how does it strike
Moments shape the hours with a mighty hammer.

II. INCANTATIONS IN THE SIGHS FOR THE SUN

All men detach themselves and become unique,
Every human being will then be like a flower, untrammelled
Every movement will be direct.
Only to be will be such delight,
we cover our faces when we think of it.
Lest our faces betray us to some untimely fiend.

-D H Lawrance

When flowers wither odour lingers in air,
Sun abides in the sighs as the waves break,
The sound rests on the floating flowers and leaves
And before I make out, you appear on the doorstep.

Thinner than me, a man…lovelier than me, a man
Flashes in your eyeballs in its subtle form,
Although you know the circumference of blue
Wherever you go the time's circle breaks in you.

When I meet you a segment of spring skies remains,
It unfurls like a new branch, a narrow path of
Time within: a fraction divides the virgin heart
Into five chambers and my entity waits to breathe.

A glow gleams the sighs from the glimpse of sun
Sun, the source of desires, sprouts up the paddy seeds,
Coiled, the desires reside in the heart,
Crossing the first step you snap a world that changes ever.
Into five chambers and my entity waits to breathe.

Spring is the cruel season. A little anguish lingers,
Some thirst without hunger under the green leaf umbrella
Our unreachable desire places a ladder downward
And gradually advances onto own self.

While climbing the steps, who knows, these extend below.
Yet another small stretch of stony steps,
Yet when you climb down one more stretch
A marvel bull stalls all your movement.

Down below an odour, a jungle of flowers, a casket of spring
Varying colour of awareness brings in variable reflections of skies
Yet another person is your endearing poet.

Some desires wither in the sun, some on the edges of the leaves,
Some desires wither with the waiving of the warm wings of a skylark.
But you can't fly despite your wonderous strivings:
Words and words you hurl at me to arrest my age.

Sound comes in cycle, gets into the heart as waves break,
Soundless desolation seeks shelter again;
All truth can delineate a vessel with a pen,
Even if you cross an ocean your throne is safe.

An odour lingers in your garden till you cognise,
Fostered childhood seeks soul's secret love;
You don't know while awaiting a little away,
The touch of your sighs opens up my skies.

You leap onto a swing in the left chamber rightside groove,
Play like a duckling in the pond with the pressure of oar from North,
From the warmth to a cool moon and frosty stars;
You shine in a sealed chamber, glitter in a radium tipped hand.

Like telescopic images your footmarks imprinted on my sighs
And at once a swing is hung
Despite the four self-effulgent children found asleep in four corners.

His blue physique flashes fervently.
And people in groups stand still.
Although you donot open the gate.
A few break open it inflicting injury on watchman.

Thinner than me a man thinner and lovelier
Becomes myself till the lashback of wind touches shore.
A sheet of water is not lost by folding,
Songs do not emanate from a sitar in carsurina trees.
Words outpaced waves, waves beneath the waves of wind
Words assume a form, mode of thought, transcribe a touch
Beneath a sheet of water swings a cowrie, an oyster.
If you don't fix your mind scenes of drama lose charm.

Spring sprinkles colours up the skies, then on your face.
Then *Radha, Lalita* and *Vishakha* enter into grooves,
Hold Krishna in a swing and close their eyes-
The waiting of cow-calf and cow women varies forthwith.

Patches of green clouds, blue clouds and arch of yellow clouds
Don't respond to your calls, and the words from your lips.
Cant hold me in tact. Despite all your compassion.
I fail to address you: "O you are my own".

Full length picture of a spirited man,
A tall *sal* tree and the mighty armed king,
Vigour hid in the folds of humanity.
A colossal figure hid in the subtle skies,
Documents and deeds of land rights hid in the strong room.
Stairs wind downwards and the plastic ropes are knotted.
You have to clutch the rope to climb beneath your skull;
The squire you can't make cut from the painstaking penance of a city,

The penance which scatters the dots of splendour;
And with the death of *Krouncha* note of grief rings in a poet's heart.
Odour lingers in flowers, a flower turns into a mum bee,
Expositions shape man and the foliage emits odour.

Another man lovelier than him you have not traced.
Another man more faithful and thinner you have not traced;
Shadows of outer objects assume varying hues within
There is a shade of difference in your face in the mirror.

Keep quiet, a lonely house in the meadows
And your words evoke echoes from a distance
Return to the walls of the cave, repeat the sounds;
The chatter boxes pause as clapping grips the middle of the stage.

Spring is the cruel -season, lovelier than you;
It scatters handful of flowers and sprinkles colours on the green earth.

Once there Lived a Prince

Only a prince, uniquely handsome,
While seeking a bride.
Lone, on a horseback in a city thoroughfare,
Lone, he chanced upon a matchless beauty,
Enticed, they eyed each other
Enticed, they waited each other.

And the prince intercepted,
"Unique glamour glitters on your limbs,
Grace of soul shines through the limbs,
Scriptural elegance is filled in words and rhythms;
Your movement is sweet without attachment.
O desireless, oh princess without blemish!
Will you nod your approval
Of one -pointed penance,
Of single -minded union of hearts?

Mum, the merchant maid returned
And the courtier put the last question:
"O *Sresthi*, o the most affluent one!
Will you gauge the depth of love
Of the prince towards your daughter?
Or will you love to prefer wrath of the Maharaja?

The daughter hit upon an idea.
She convinced her father and sought eight days,
Sought permission to face the prince in a battle of wits:
"If he nods his approval
Why should I remain speechless?"
The daughter toyed with the idea
That human body is nourished with juices from the food.
The daughter went to the palace in a palanquin
Eight days after. And the prince exclaimed:
"Oh what a look! That day you walked like a moon!"

Beaconing at the eight vessels of excretions
The daughter said " the beauty of body, the enticing form,
Lies under the vessels;
That magical spell stalls your steps
When you are out to take a dip
See my skeleton form, see me in public"
The prince declined. Only a silence reigned the courtroom.
 * * *

Is food a swan which swims across the tank?
Where is the glamour on the limbs without food?
Plum is pleasant and sweet when tasted.
Plum is gnawed by the teeth and the cup of juice
Drip dropping in the heart enhances the elegance on the skin,
Yet its beauty ends up in the channel of *Apana*.

Flower wither emitting odour into the air,
As you take leave of me someone meanders along.

III- BRIDAL BAND TO THE OTHER SIDE OF THE WOODS

O the mind, mind has mountains, cliffs of fall
    Frightful, sheer, no man fathomed.
        Nor does long our small
    Durance deal with that steep or deep.
                      -Hopkins

A procession winds through the woods with palanquin and
bridal carriage,
A procession spearheads with the drums, the trumpets and the
bugles,
Followers, tuned to the inklings from the bandmaster dancing;
Can't gauge the meaning of the next scene,
The next rhythm and the ensuing dialogue:
Yet a silent exchange of words moves from mind to mind.

The rhythm of dance in the feet without the rules of grammar,
The pollens of joy in the hands,
The mementoes of garlands, sandal paste, camphor and scented oil
Smeared on the forehead.
Is some spell of magic cast on the jungle path?
Rows and rows of *MAHUL* and *KARANJ* trees,
Moonbeam like the silver ink.
And the tail end of the letters here and there.

The moonlit night of April and the bridal party
Winding forward to the otherside of woods,
Nobody knows the other's desire, scans all that
Half familiar people expeditious, languishing in an exact tune.

Nobody ever thinks where is his own place.

An abode is not located in the woods, land or water,
A bird's nest tossing about in the swing of air alone.

You have not viewed the face of the bride at all
You have not queried about groom's qualification,

You have not scrutinised the sister-in-law,
You have not scanned the burden of the daughter-in-law's words,
You don't know the moth-in-law's rasp-tongued ire,
You don't know the father-in-law's deft decoy,
Without gauging all these, you think of relationship lovelier than heaven.

The bandmaster dances in the front, dances in tune with the flashes of music;
Weighs your beat with the rolling eyes of an alcoholic stupor.
You are infatuated with the dance or music or exhibitionism
Striving, seeking pleasure or earning easy eclat!

Band moulds the turning of the trumpet and slowly the sound of bugle,
From clarionet emanates the trumpet of a pet elephant;
Such in your mind that whatever you watch or listen
Its wave runs through the breath, a sloka turns into plain couplet.

Wind has its abode… it builds and descends from the skies;
Descends on earth, whereupon I watch the sunrise;
Glance the embers though the gaps of leaves;
I, an ageing man, in your eyes make out the entity
I measure out my movement and mind as a lark,
Those carry the palanquin melt like dream,
A riot of dance and songs shrinks on the other side of the horizon,
Moon hangs in the sky like a dead hare,
The flower vase glitters when dawn peeps through the door.

Nothing to be restless, only a bell tolls from the temple,
First comes the sound, next the incantations;
To the open window a gush of song from the *tanpura*,

Sung by a blindman. Then a gust of wind hooks your ears-
Wind through the wings of the butterflies-
Sunshine glimmers like *champak*, squares of gold;
Glitters in the air. Semblance of sun in dewdrop.

Watch the image in the mirror but don't stare at air.
If the golden oriole spreads its wings-a handful of emptiness,
Its wings cover up undiminishing silence of a saint.
You tread on the path of violence and perfidy on the earth
Unless you fly out you cant comprehend its blue imagery.

Lone, in the inn you walk and look at the garden.
You have hair-do and you watch the shadows of skies.
You stir up the three traits, mix the three colours in the tea spoon
While chanting with agility you watch for silence or your image
in my eyeball.

I see too many deals to delve into the meaning of a scenery;
The wayward child jumps a wall and places dislodged branches.
Then they gather to vie with each other in a race.
They touch the sketched river and their boats float with the
morning gulp.

If you simulate anger after longing an object twice,
The song from the radio reminds *"Jeevan patra Mo…"*
The inner joy overflows with sweet mutterings
Throwing the papers away if you leave in a huff-
Who imprints a thumb on your pocket, a red red rose!
You have greed for shadows, on looking into the shadows
You find these divided In the grass and the sand,
Quiet you come back, quiet as the hands of the dawn
Stretching wide over the fields and bowers.

While watching the scenery you become part of it
Unaware, your eyes measure out the skies and deepen;
A reply to my letter unleashes storm with ink and love.
Thoughtful you build a barricade for the confined mind.

Sunshine of *Tecoma* flowers floats silver squares in air,
From leaves hang the sunbeam wings of the butterflies.

Sun behind a patch of cloud glitters like silver plate.
Rock grains, smoke and lightning flash in the sky
Despite all strength the mad horses can't move a wheel
Or the charioteer. And on all sides the fear of soul is set.

All that Penelope knits during the day unties at night.
Will ever the sprinkling of colours shape a picture?
So with the *MANJUATI* leaves you will wrap your flowerlike palm
You will make the stars twinkle when evening is spread.

Listening to some glibing words the children in groups
Will run in varied modes in the village roads.
They will throw away tottered clothes,
Dragon flies, butterflies on the sandy lanes, oleanders and *asoka*
They will jump from the veranda, a distorted symphony.
You are in the inn and the settling sun is towards your left
On the fight the moon is up: your plams flank the opposite directions.
And you stand still; still in front of me.

Outpacing the thousand and thousand years you appear
No trace of wound in your feet, no dust around your neck and hands,
Easy was the coming together in the first evening,
You questioned at the doorstep with a smile; "Who are you"?

Man who has not recognised his mind, stares at his physique
And explores an image in the mirror.
On the desolate brim of the well Dipu, sits all the night.
Sits with a bamboo flute at his waist, sees his reflections.

Whomsoever a child watches his images dances at interval
Whomsoever you shower love his web of intimacy holds you invisibly,
Yet the condemnations elucidate in you the rights to live!
Therefore you hang a swing, clothe the clay toys
With multi-coloured pieces , place them in the moonlit night
Wind tosses your entity or the sighs of April
Touch your cheek as you clutch the pillow of the baby.

Something is Rotten....

Something is rotten in the state. Therefore, the misfortune,
And the prince notices the shadow of the apparition against the wall.
Lure for some wicked deeds waits for revenge.
On the low wall platform raised in the garden
You love but you don't drop me letters..,
How does sin accrue from the relationship with a minister?
It is always better for you to be killed in toeing the track of *swadharma*.
If you cling to prayer with folded hands, prayer for other's faith,
Waves cann't calm the roar of sea;
There is no other way except breaking yourself.

Although you recognise the kith and kin
Although you have a killer's ego
I have a question about the worship of the deserving.
I have a question about infatuation in mind.
While I go on seeking you your arrow like finger
Points to my heart where your lac-sealed letter lies:
'where do you dwell? Within or infront of me?
In the eyes of the horses? Or in the red/blue scarfs ?
In the chariot or under the wheel? '

Tearing the veil of time with pointed shoes
Soldiers come rushing towards me
The silver-bordered back cover of horses dazzle into the distance,
The acrimony gaining in strength
Or all the arrow points will tear my heart
O Lord, I surrender to you
You are the devotes dovecot, a friend to the surrendered.

* * *

A night in the inn. You did not have a wink of sleep
Who is the third person at the centre of the invisible?
When the morning teapot in is shared there is a 'surplus void'.
Who is the third person at the round table?
As you don't know him you light up a lantern in daytime.
Sit for a charting if your mind does not fluctuate,
Earth looks like a bride in front of the sky.
Don the hem of *sari* at the parting line of hair.
Gaze at the horizon that looks like a taintless half circle,
A procession winds through the woods with palanquin and bridal carriage.

IV. ON READING THE APHORISMS

I think continually of thou who were truly great Who from the womb, remembered the soul's history. Through corridors of light where the hours are suns, Endless and singing.

- **Stephen Spender**

Only a coward asks;" Is it safe?"
A greedy man questions, "What's the gain for me?"
A vain- glorious queries, "Shall I earn fame?"
Instinct interpolates: " Is there happiness ?"
And conscience exlpores: "Is this the truth?'

On reading the aphorisms connotations turn heavy.
Dove and the hawk sit on my shoulders
The two in front of the king balance their weight.
Sometimes, the planks waver left and right.
After your limb is chopped off soul triggers fresh fireworks.

Neither doubt grabs your nor dilemma
The rope of desire does not cling to your waist
Not like the border of a cloth,
There is no envy, no pride, no ego, no wanton greed
There is no politics inside the temple, the sanctum sanctorium sparkles.

Rishyashringa in the Boat, in the Palace

Famine stalked *Angadesh* and cracks appeared
The stream became slim
The king *Lomapad* queried, 'Have you any solution?'
And the priests said:
"If the wise in the knowledge of soul par excellence,
The brilliant and the apt in penance
Rishyashringa steps into this kingdom
It will rain."
The king called for the minister,
Asked to bring *RIshyashringa* from the monastery of *Vivandaka*,
"Send a band of beauty queens from the city
Send them sharp to mitigate the pangs of hungers
Of our crying crowds
O sky! Sprinkle the water of shanti!"

Bedecking the boat lively as a garden
Beauty queens went to the monk *Vivandaka*
They tied the boat to a rope, took it to *Ashram.*

Unfamiliar with the elegance of women,
Unheard of their words,
Thrilled they thought of the norms of playing host.
Identifying the form of his self emanating from penance.
He failed to discern man from woman
And washed the feet with holy water.

Yet another day.... Yet when *Vivandaka* was out from his garden
Out to gather the fruits and roots with care
The beauty queens came from the artificial garden
And spoke softly:
"How enticing is our garden, please step in without delay".

As *Rishyashringa* stepped into the boat
They untied the ropes
And the women oared towards the city,
The garden looked enchanting, up with the feast of dance and songs.
The beauty queens led *Rishyasringa* to the king *Lomapada*
At the king's behest the king of the monks sank into a sea of joy.
Rain was dripping down in joy in *Angadesh*,
Shrouds of clouds danced in the sky in ecstasy.

Rivers were full, the ponds and the people's aspirations
Pinning full faith on the *Tapaswi* the king offered
Shanta, his daughter of soul born of Truth, in marriage.

Droplets of gold drenched the soil of *Angadesh*,
Rivers turned turbulent, screams of clouds rent from skies.

*   *   *

The sun pours down murky stream on the wings of a dove,
The verse and refrain of your song ring up leaves and flowers.

The aphorisms, experiences and the advices of the priests, monks
Keep vigil over the heart like a cobra,
As you fix your look on a particular point
You open up gradually and expand like a circle.

From an incident in a short story truth is clearer
If you see the face once it is a symmetry of lines-
Times which are worked out like a soon end in courage-

And in me you gather strength as my own.
If you walk into water the lotus blossoms,
Weight of ochre clothes weigh the skies around shoulders, neck;
Light footed *Gopis* cross over the flood water
But the burden of palmleaf drags the pandit down to sifting sand.

The prince understands the pledge of Faerie Queen,
Humble and undaunted fighter aims at transcendence;
A foe in vanquished at the first gate and says *Yudhisthir*,
'Do you know the news of the world, know about time in a culdron.

You love again and pine for the return of that day,
Love the height of a man without measuring the shadow;
You have pledge in your mind about the Holy Grail;
You can listen to the language of the heart of your neighbour in silence.

You pin faith on the creeper to watch the maiden rain,
Unfolding flowers in ecstasy, bringing fertility to ambient earth,
The calf and the cow, the deer, the peacock and the peahen
Form the picturesque islands on the fringe of *Tamala* fields,

The wall is a wall changing to your faith, the mirror against it
Hangs from a nail to the knee, Your face flashes every morning
Like a rising sun and the thunder turns into a swan
In the lake of your heart for whose joy whose curse?

Sunshine cannot shun the wings of dove, fly out;
Memory and wisdom strike balance , shadows float.

Verses read in childhood flash on the screen for the middle aged,
Nanny's tales act as open sesame to quell the grand daughter
An ass at the doorstep of the fort, horseman wielding a sword
Oh! What a dangerous measure is to lay by things !

The monkey species clamour to gain favour of *RAMA*.
A faithful man is content with a wink,
Though a stranger, I stretch my hands towards you
When I see you clutching the roots and dangling at the well.

Speak less, words on the wings of the wind
Creep up, creep up towards the creepers of siads.
Lazy like tangled beasts, yet fearless,
Do you ever query where conscience is the quandary ?

Someone, someone before the closure of the last scene
Of drama gives out inkling to change the feeling of audience
And this sets the minds at rest.

Your wisdom is a closed museum
None is there to witness what have you picked up and from where.
A dove to your left and a hawk to your right
The weighing scale strikes a balance when you chop off your limbs.

A tiny temple inside a temple and a sanctuary
Monument within the precincts of the sanctuary speaks volumes,
Reveals the secrets but no cries. Still you can hear
With the ears against the walls: the wail of the soul.

* * *

Once upon a time…while hunting his prey,
Unquiet with the thirst, Maharaja *Parikshit* wandered
And wandered till he chanced upon a Maharshi in an Ashram.
He prayed and waited at his feet but to no avail.
In a feat of wrath he flung at the bow-end a dead cobra.
It entwined round the neck, a long garland of flowers.
On seeing how the meditative mood of the master has repulsed
Sringa, a crafty *Bramhachari*, cursed the king for his childish egotism.

Death raising its hood as *Takshyak* will sting you,
Just after seven days you will be doomed.

Maharshi called for a messenger, apprised the king:
Leave aside the elegant couch, listen to the tales of *Bhagabat* for a week.

* * *

When you listen to the slokas the burden of these
Turns heavy gradually, wisdom and science outweighs.
You scan the lines which outshine like burning wicks,
Shining waves streak down the mind.
If you come down the sandy bylane, if you come,
You bring a palmful of fruits and flowers with faith in your heart !

V. COME IN, ONCE AGAIN

I said to my soul, be still and wait without hope.
For hope would be hope for the wrong thing, wait without love.
For love would be love of the lwrong thing, there is yet faith.
But the faith and the love and the hope are all in the waiting.
                                                    - **T S Eliot**

While counting the heads on the otherside of the river,
Well aware of the boatman's call
They don't count their own.
Yet another man is not traced
Yet another of matching height:
Simple and straight like us/like us he speaks less.

If you beckon me in dream at the dawn,
If you hint at the road leading to you,
If you assure that a passer-by accompanied by
Friends, wife and children, or moving alone,
Does not swerve from the way,
You call me, "You can come concealing coins of desires in a bundle of clothes."

Your pull weighs heavy from the physique to the vital air,
Your two eyes pull us beyond the mind;
Have I learnt to fly out, have I learnt
To remove a slab of rugged stone,
Have I learnt to cross over a thorny river?

You flash everyday and everyday I repent.
I write a letter and lay it nearby.
I search for the address forgetting that you told,
"The first step is self confidence and resurging awareness."

Encased in the still chamber of heart, your name an ornament.
There is casket within the chest and within the casket

The radium-tipped hand, while I am asleep, rotates and ticks on my chest.

Whenever I look, you flash. You flash behind a mirror
Sometimes kneeling , sometimes on the cover of a notebook;
Your winkless eyes flash *yoga mudra* in absolute stillness,
The more I gaze at you the more you gaze again.

Patches of the floating clouds have deep blue robes within,
The sea of compassion spits foam and keeps on floating your throne.
Do you leave inklings for the lonely passer-by in the darkness
While he seeks his way do you send a shaft of lightning?

When I measure a foot and tread inch by inch
My fingers are held in your fist,
Oh, who holds me tight…air or earth or man,
The one -pointed entreaty or the amazing courage.

Sun shaped up the skies and a ladder in void,
Crops cling to the earth like the life:
The nectarine drops studded on clouds, beads of sweats on the forehead
I trace as I go on seeking you at the core of divine desire,
You watch me and call for surrendering all my intellect,
All the heart and remaining years,
The sweet aspirations;
O grant me the remaining possibilities:

Rows of trees on the roadside resemble a drill-class
Rows of trees hint at the way ahead.
A priest with luggage on his shoulders,

A yellow apron and a red napkin.
In the crowd there is a stream which can lead you to temple alone.
The nearer you are I remember you all the more,
I recite the slokas when wake up …. *Atmatattwa*
I recite during bath the glory of the *Ganga, Yamuna, the Sangam*,
With a palmful of water the heaven, the earth and the blue lark are washed.

A throne in the heart and jasmine garland entwined round the wrist.
The moon and the sun basking in eyeballs with the glory of bliss,
The deity of a scripture evokes sweet response in ears.
For knitting in the fleeting time moments run into eternity.

Lure for you is more, more from the heart and more from the eyes,
The incessant tears flow out hands of rain here and there.
With the advent of *Aashad* clouds go berserk,
Swinging they dance on the oars of storm.

Enduring the sorrows turns out to be great virtue,
Search with a headful of feeling, search with knowledge,
Or an inquiry into the nature of Truth
A reply echoes don't you know I live everywhere,
From the handful of dust you gather, a deity you trace.

Frenzied youth is quiet with your power of glory,
Quiet with the practice of penance, repetition of habits and love;
Quiet with the quest in dancing, quiet at sitting under the feet continually
Uninterrupted is your search and there is not a speck of dust on the mountain path.

Moon flings the darkness of mind into the shadow
In a night of *Ashadh*;
Whose light swims across the lake of heart,
 whose image is quiet and murky….
And the mind is brighter than wisdom and lovelier than joy.
Steps and steps of moonbeam, stone edges washed by rain.
Dots and dots of grace of bliss;
When we go on exploring his blessings
We become ourselves the sanctuaries
The earth emitting holy odour.

Pilgrims here and there: all looks switch over to His eyes in a moment.
All looks roll to touch the waves of bliss,
Swastik, vessel or nude images, wheel or the trident.
The elevated verandahs reflect the gains of rare penance.

Altars For Lamps At Every Doorstep

Now move forward lest you may be lost
Come entwining the hands among the groups of women,
A newly wedded walks with the veil swinging under eye-lids;
How can you see Him in your inner sanctum?
A lion before the steps safeguard your virtue.
Shoes at the entrance speak of the haughty ego,
If you push these aside and advance
An elephant blind with infatuation is killed,
The dome is donned with potraits.

A lotus, a conch and a bow craved on the wooden doors,
Arranging the scenes one after another you are a bad poet;
Yagnakunda, Garuda or the sleepless *Nandi*
Impart you the message to build the decade of sacrifice.

Yet another entrance, two angels holding the garlands
Guard the threshold, stars and planets and satellites.
Do they hang from the skies or dangle in space above the hand
While I move round your entity stretches on the right.
The door keepers at the fourth gate stare
While we stare at you,
You walk in full swing swirling like a stream.
Nothing was in the hand lent now it holds
Flowers, perfumery, earthen lamps. Quatrain on the tip of your tongue.

* * *

Close the eyes and explore the blue range of clouds
Atop the altar of heart, the throne studded with gems;
Studded these tie up the subtle awareness.
All at once, His glimmer opens the eyelids.

Time ago you were one with the log or the lingam,
Time ago you were swimming swifter than a fish deep in the water of Gandak.
Yet the lotus covered on the stone, the *Ananta Sayana*-
Sink, however, deeper in me sooner you surface.

Descend into my streams of tears, flash on my thoughtless forehead.
Foster me in love as I have come to know
There are fears of storms and worms before the flowers unfold ;
Kindly put your signature on the blue leaf.

When did you build the stone wall? And the wing the wood
Carve out my body as a chariot? Become a witness to it – its charioteer!
Alters donned with earthen lamps, *chitra* lamps, *natya* lamps and *Ratna* lamps
Unveil the limits of awareness and stretch you on ten directions.
You stand out placing hands on the northern and southern directions,
And the ocean in front of you rolls on waves on the eastern side.

Come from the Omkar, the wheel or the crescent/
The cross, the fire, the trident or from the bed of the ocean of milk.
I see your reflection I see the sky from my soul/
The skies scan air and the sun and the clouds,
Your inspiration concentrates on the crops/
The earth is the divine expression of your thought.
While counting the people on the other side of the river,

Well aware of the boatman's call,
They don't count their own.
Yet another man is not traced,
Yet another of matching height
Simple and straight like us/like us a chatter-box.
When the boatman counts the heads on the other side of the river,
You are traced in the eyes of others.

***

Black Eagle Books

www.blackeaglebooks.org
info@blackeaglebooks.org

Black Eagle Books, an independent publisher, was founded as a nonprofit organization in April, 2019. It is our mission to connect and engage the Indian diaspora and the world at large with the best of works of world literature published on a collaborative platform, with special emphasis on foregrounding Contemporary Classics and New Writing.

www.ingramcontent.com/pod-product-compliance
Lightning Source LLC
Chambersburg PA
CBHW020548080526
44583CB00013B/1052